Introduction

Horses are beautiful animals, so many children like to draw them, But they don't know where and how to start.

This book will teach children and beginners how to draw horses step by step with a simple drawing method.

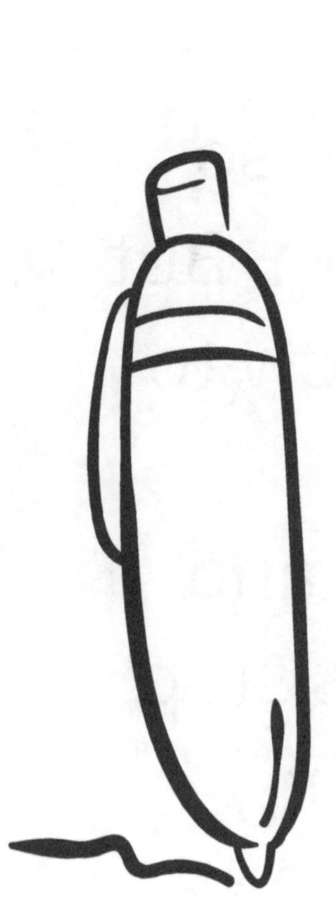

Matrials Needed:

- ruler
- pencil
- marker
- eraser

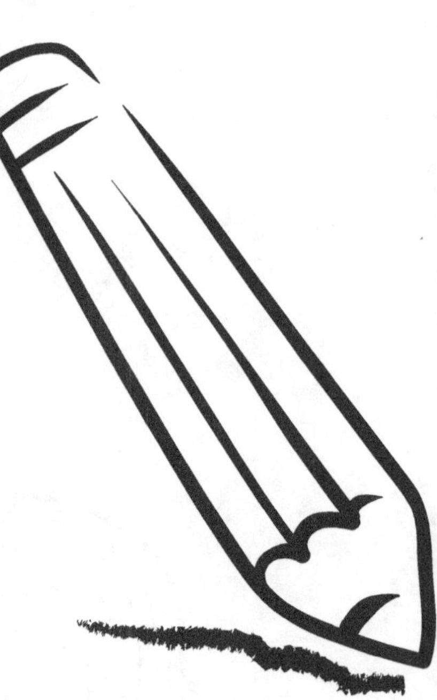

FIRST, LET'S START WITH SOME TRACING EXERCISES TO IMPROVE OUR SKILLS, THEN WE WILL MOVE TO A STEP BY STEP GUIDE TO DRAWING HORSES.

TRACE AND COLOR

TRACE AND COLOR

TRACE AND COLOR

TRACE AND COLOR

TRACE AND COLOR

TRACE AND COLOR

TRACE AND COLOR

TRACE AND COLOR

TRACE AND COLOR

TRACE AND COLOR

TRACE AND COLOR

TRACE AND COLOR

TRACE AND COLOR

TRACE AND COLOR

TRACE AND COLOR

NOW WE ARE READY TO START DRAWING OUR FIRST HORSE!

IT IS ESSENTIAL TO START DRAWING THE HORSE ALL OVER AGAIN AT EACH STEP TO GET USED TO DRAWING

START BY DRAWING THE HEAD

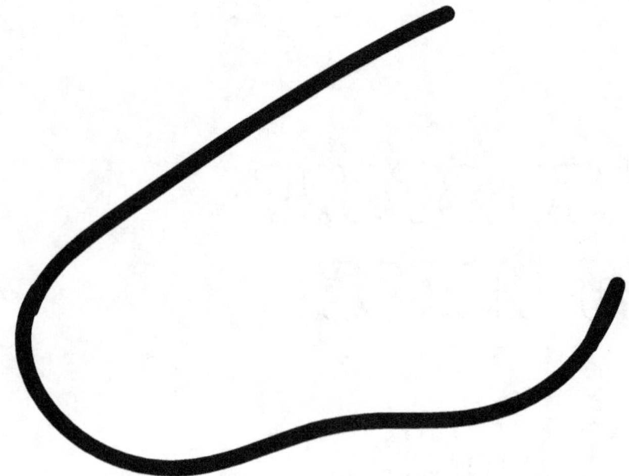

YOUR TURN

DRAW THE EARS

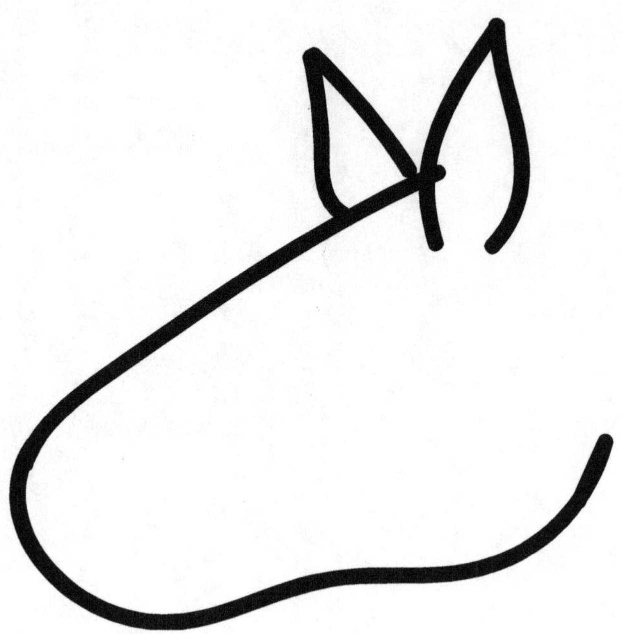

YOUR TURN

DRAW THE NECK

YOUR TURN

DRAW THE LEGS

YOUR TURN

DRAW THE BACK

YOUR TURN

COMPLETE DRAWING THE LEGS

YOUR TURN

NOW DRAW THE HORSE'S TAIL AND HOOF

YOUR TURN

DRAW THE MANE

YOUR TURN

DRAW THE FACE

YOUR TURN

NOW OUR CUTE HORSE IS
READY ! YOU CAN COLOR IT

YOUR TURN

LETS TRY TO DRAW ANOTHER TYPE OF HORSES

DRAW THE BACK

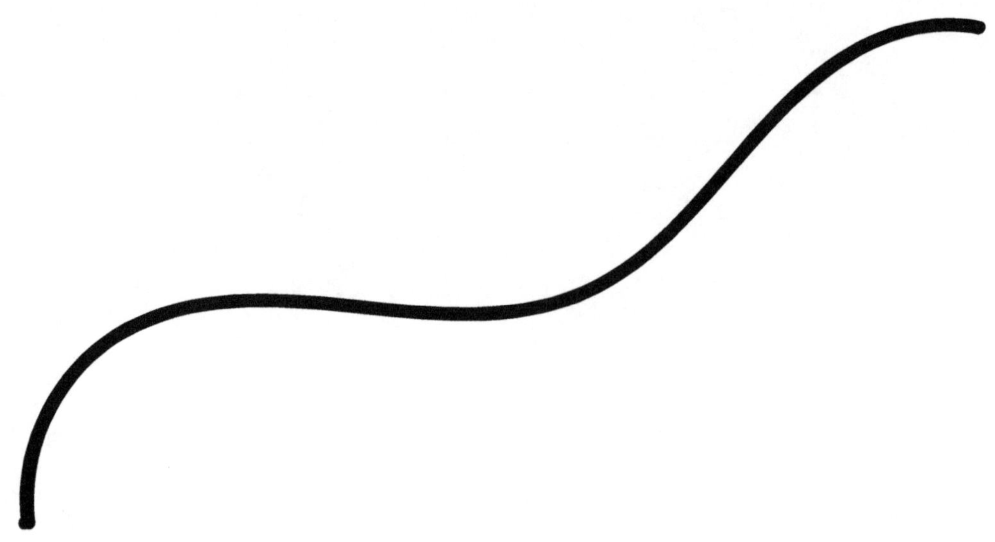

YOUR TURN

DRAW THE HEAD

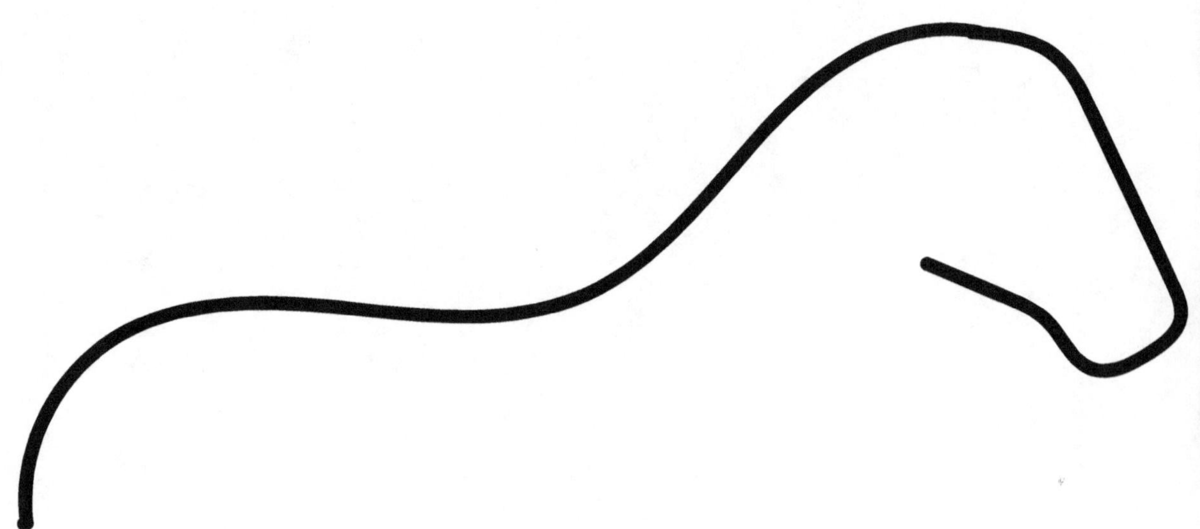

YOUR TURN

DRAW THE NECK AND THE CHEST

YOUR TURN

DRAW THE FRONT LEG

YOUR TURN

DRAW BACK LEG

YOUR TURN

YOUR TURN

CONTINUE DRAWING THE LEGS

YOUR TURN

CONTINUE DRAWING THE LEGS

YOUR TURN

DRAW THE MANE

YOUR TURN

DRAW THE TAIL

YOUR TURN

ERASE THE INSIDE LINES

YOUR TURN

OUR HORSE IS READY!
COLOR IT

YOUR TURN

CUTE HORSE COLORING PAGES